My Science Library

The Wonderful Water Cycle

by Kimberly M. Hutmacher

Science Content Editor:
Shirley Duke

Rourke
Educational Media

rourkeeducationalmedia.com

Science Content Editor: Shirley Duke holds a bachelor's degree in biology and a master's degree in education from Austin College in Sherman, Texas. She taught science in Texas at all levels for twenty-five years before starting to write for children. Her science books include *You Can't Wear These Genes, Infections, Infestations, and Diseases, Enterprise STEM, Forces and Motion at Work, Environmental Disasters,* and *Gases.* She continues writing science books and also works as a science content editor.

www.rourkeeducationalmedia.com

Photo credits: Cover © Anneka, W. Scott, Yuriy Kulyk, 26kot, Matthijs Wetterauw; Pages 2/3 © dpaint; Pages 4/5 © Arvind Balaraman, Willyam Bradberry, Anneka, Rob Marmion, Jorg Hackemann, Len Green; Pages 6/7 © Juriah Mosin, Brenda Carson, Kostyantyn Ivanyshen Pages 8/9 © somchaij, Kameel4u, agoxa, Alex Staroseltsev; Pages 10/11 © Daniel Taeger, paint, MarinaMariya; Pages 12/13 © John Dorado, Blue Door Education; Pages 14/15 © dvande, Patrickma; Pages 16/17 © KIKETXO, africa924; Pages 18/19 © Jan S., ACID RAIN IMAGE; Pages 20/21 © ncn18

Editor: Kelli Hicks

My Science Library series produced by Blue Door Publishing, Florida for Rourke Educational Media.

Library of Congress PCN Data

Hutmacher, Kimberly M.
 The Wonderful Water Cycle / Kimberly M. Hutmacher.
   p. cm. -- (My Science Library)
 ISBN 978-1-61810-104-4 (hard cover - English)(alk. paper)
 ISBN 978-1-61810-237-9 (soft cover - English)
 ISBN 9781618103666 (e-Book - English)
 ISBN 9781631550607 (hard cover - Spanish)(alk. paper)
 ISBN 9781627173391 (soft cover - Spanish)
 ISBN 9781627175494 (e-Book - Spanish)
Library of Congress Control Number: 2011943576

Rourke Educational Media
Printed in the United States of America,
North Mankato, Minnesota

Also Available as:

rourkeeducationalmedia.com

customerservice@rourkeeducationalmedia.com
PO Box 643328 Vero Beach, Florida 32964

Table of Contents

Water, Water, Everywhere!

Where is water? The question should be, where isn't water? Three-quarters of Earth is blanketed by water! People, plants, and animals are all made up mostly of water, and every living thing needs water to survive.

We use water every day for drinking, bathing, and flushing toilets. Water is used for cleaning, generating power, and for **recreation**. Water is very important for **agriculture**, too.

SaltWater vs Fresh

Most of Earth's water isn't usable in everyday life. Over 96 percent of our water is saltwater which can't be used for cooking and drinking.

Sixty percent of the world's fresh water withdrawals go toward irrigation. Large-scale farming couldn't provide food for the world's population without irrigation systems.

Many farmers are able to get all of the water their crops need from rainfall, but in drier areas, farmers use other ways to get water to their fields. They use a process called **irrigation** to pump water from other sources like lakes and rivers through ditches, canals, and pipes.

Did you know that when you take a sip from the water fountain at school or from the tap at home, you're not getting new water? The water you're drinking has been on Earth forever! All of the water we have now is all of the water we ever had and ever will have. Our water travels in a never-ending process called the **water cycle**.

The water you drink has been around since the age of dinosaurs!

Water Magic

Water is **matter**. Matter is anything that has mass and takes up space. It can be a solid, liquid, or gas. Did you know that water can be all three? Water can change form. Water is not always a liquid. It can freeze into solid ice. It can boil and become a gas.

The Three States of Matter

solid

liquid

gas

Puddles of water dry up on warm, sunny days. Does the water in the puddles just disappear? No! The water **evaporates**. This means that the water is absorbed into the air around it. Tiny water particles called **molecules** are in motion. They bounce off one another. Some of these moving molecules hit and fly free. They move into the air. This forms **water vapor**. Adding heat makes them move faster. That's why evaporation is faster on warm days.

If you own a fish, you probably change part of the water in your fish bowl each week. When you do this, you probably notice that some of the water you added the week before is gone. Where does it go? That's right! It evaporates!

Making Rain

When air that's full of water vapor cools, it changes the gas back to a liquid in the form of tiny water droplets. This is **condensation**. Water continues to condense, forming the clouds in our sky.

When the clouds get so large and heavy that the air can't support them anymore, the water falls as **precipitation**, more commonly known as rain, sleet, snow, or hail.

Condensation

You don't have to look to faraway clouds to see condensation in action. As your glass of water cools the air around it, there is less heat energy for individual water molecules to move around. These molecules join together, forming the water droplets on the outside of your glass. We call this condensation.

The Water Cycle

The water cycle is the continuous movement of water on, in, and above Earth. It has four parts:

Evaporation. The Sun heats up water in oceans, rivers, and lakes, causing the water to turn into vapor that rises into the air.

Condensation. Once in the air, the vapor cools and liquifies, forming clouds.

Precipitation. When so much water condenses that the air can't hold it anymore, the heavy clouds allow the water to fall back to Earth in the form of rain, hail, sleet, or snow.

Collection. The water may fall back into the oceans, rivers, or lakes, or it may end up on land. If it ends up on land, it may soak into Earth, becoming part of its groundwater, or it may run over the soil and collect back into the oceans, rivers, and lakes. This is where the cycle starts over again.

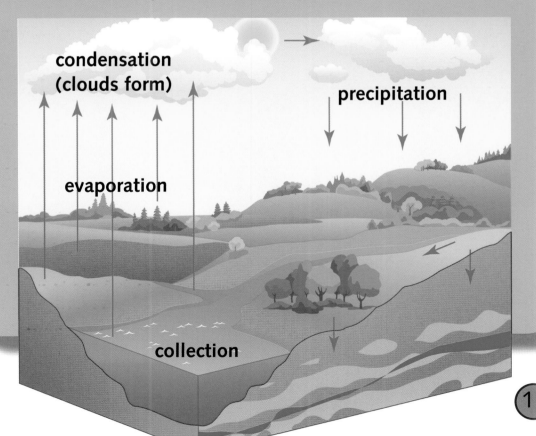

condensation (clouds form)

precipitation

evaporation

collection

What Happens to Rainwater?

Some rainwater seeps into rocks and soil underground. **Reservoirs** are man-made places where water is collected and stored for future use. Some water flows into rivers and some collects in reservoirs, where it can be pumped out for human use.

The reservoir with the largest water capacity in the United States is Lake Mead. It lies over the borders of Nevada and Colorado.

The water in the reservoirs isn't clean, though. It's full of mud, dangerous chemicals, germs, and trash. The water has to be made clean enough to drink.

This water is pumped into a water treatment plant. Machines at treatment plants filter out the solid waste in the water, and special cleaning chemicals are added to kill germs.

Aquifers

An aquifer is an area of saturated underground rock through which water easily moves. This rock includes sandstone, broken limestone, sand, and gravel. A hole called a well is drilled into the ground and into the aquifer. Water from the aquifer either flows out or is pumped out for use.

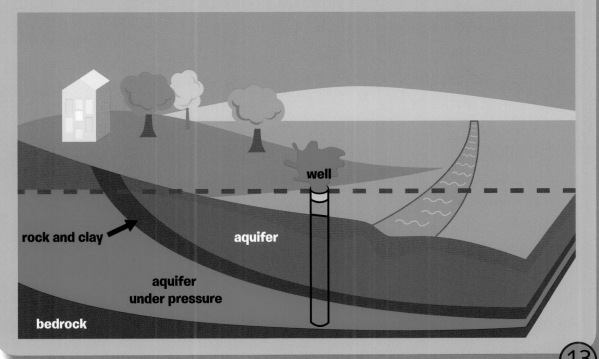

rock and clay

aquifer

aquifer under pressure

well

bedrock

Washed Away!

When you flush your toilet or let water run down your sink drain, the water isn't clean anymore. It's now called sewage. **Sewage** travels through another maze of pipes back to the treatment plant to be cleaned and filtered and made safe all over again.

Sewage Treatment

1. Used water from the community is pumped through pipes and enters the sewers.
2. Water flows into grit chambers where larger particles sink to bottom.
3. It flows into primary settling tank.
4. Solids are removed from the water and are reprocessed and used for fertilizer.
5. Water runs over beds of rocks for filtration.
6. Chemicals are added to kill germs.
7. The water is aerated.
8. Water is effluent. It is treated once more and put back into local streams and rivers.

Scientists and inventors work hard to come up with practical and inexpensive ways to purify water in developing countries. One interesting innovation is a straw that filters water before it touches lips. Another is a bicycle that not only hauls water but also uses kinetic energy to filter it.

Solar water disinfection (SODIS) is one way to treat contaminated water. Using a special bottle, the water sits in the sun for six hours, allowing the radiation to kill diarrhea-causing germs.

Water Towers

If you live in or have ever driven through a small town, you've probably seen a water tower. A water tower is an elevated structure that stores and pressurizes water for distribution.

Drought!

A drought is a long period of time (usually months or years) without rain. Drought is determined by a lack of precipitation and the change in the balance of the average amount of rain and evaporation. Droughts can lead to crop damage, water shortages, dust storms, and wildfires.

Long periods of drought and evaporation can cause lakes and river beds to dry up.

Surviving Drought

Populations can and do survive drought. Rain barrels are used to collect rainwater. Irrigation systems are used to redirect water for crops and livestock. People also dig wells in attempts to find new sources of groundwater.

In areas of many African countries, people walk for miles to fetch fresh water from wells.

Wasting and Pollution

○○○○○○○○○○○○○○○○○○○○○○○○○○

Almost seven billion people on Earth have to share the world's water supply in order to survive. Many people don't have access to clean drinking water. We have to be careful not to waste it. Every day, people let leaky faucets drip and leave the water running when it's not necessary.

About one-sixth of the world's population doesn't have access to clean drinking water.

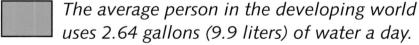 *The average person in the developing world uses 2.64 gallons (9.9 liters) of water a day.*

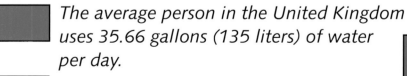 *The average person in the United Kingdom uses 35.66 gallons (135 liters) of water per day.*

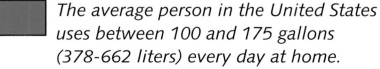 *The average person in the United States uses between 100 and 175 gallons (378-662 liters) every day at home.*

Water Consumption Around The World

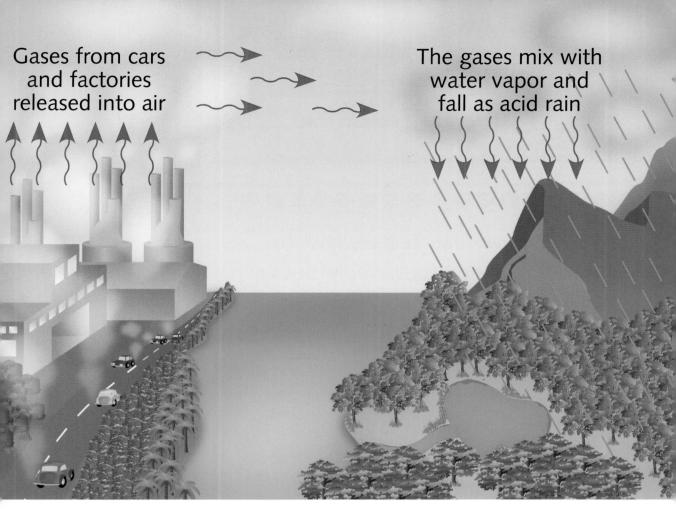

Gases from cars and factories released into air

The gases mix with water vapor and fall as acid rain

Acid rain makes water toxic to many aquatic animals. It damages the leaves on trees.

We need to work to keep our water supply clean. Too often, careless people litter our waterways with things like dropped wrappers and forgotten water bottles. Chemicals in the smoke from vehicles and factories attach to water vapor in the air, causing more **acid rain** to fall to Earth. We don't want our water supply to become so dirty that people and wildlife can't use it and take pleasure in it.

Caring for our Wonderful Water

Some governments have laws to help protect the water supply, but we all have to do our part. **Conserve** water by turning off the water faucet when you don't need the water right away. Take quick showers, and turn off the water while you soap up. When doing dishes, fill the sink with water. Turn the water off while washing. Don't run the water again until you're ready to rinse.

The United States Environmental Protection Agency (EPA) works for and enforces laws meant to protect our nation's air, water, and soil from harmful pollutants.

Many areas have laws that restrict when and how much lawns can be watered. In order to conserve water, most people water in the morning because there is less evaporation.

Don't Litter!

In fact, you could help a lot by taking a few hours each week to pick up garbage along a beach or around a lake.

It's important that we take care to keep our water clean and use it wisely. We want our limited fresh water supply to be used and enjoyed forever by everyone!

Show What You Know

1. Name at least three uses for water.

2. How does water change from one form to another?

3. Explain what you can do to conserve our water supply and keep it clean.

Glossary

acid rain (ass-ID rayn): rain formed when factory smoke pollutes the air with chemicals that attach to water vapor that may cause damage to the environment

agriculture (AG-ruh-kul-chur): having to do with farming

condensation (kon-den-SAY-shuhn): droplets of water brought together in the air by cooling

conserve (kuhn-SURV): to preserve something or keep it from being wasted or lost

evaporates (i-VAP-uh-rates): changes to a vapor or a gas by heat

irrigation (ihr-uh-GAY-shuhn): bringing water to land by ditches, canals, or pipes

matter (MAT-ur): anything that has mass and takes up space

molecules (MOL-uh-kyoolz): small units of matter

precipitation (pri-sip-i-TAY-shuhn): rain, sleet, hail, or snow that falls from the sky

recreation (rek-ree-AY-shuhn): the sports, hobbies, or forms of exercise that people play for fun

reservoirs (REZ-ur-vwarz): places where rainwater is collected for later use

sewage (SOO-ij): wastewater carried away by pipes to be made clean

water cycle (WAW-tur SYE-kuhl): the continuous journey water takes falling from clouds, evaporating in the air, and condensing back into clouds

water vapor (WAW-tur VAY-pur): water in the form of a gas

Index

Websites to Visit

water.epa.gov/learn/kids/drinkingwater/kids_4-8.cfm

www.sciencenewsforkids.org/2011/06/swirling-seas-of-plastic-trash/

www.kids.nationalgeographic.com/kids/stories/spacescience/
   water-bottle-pollution/

About the Author

Kimberly M. Hutmacher is the author of 24 books for children. She loves to research science topics and share what she learns. She also enjoys sharing her love of writing with audiences of all ages.

Meet The Author!
www.meetREMauthors.com